ORIGIN AND HISTORY OF THE ENGLISH SPRINGER SPANIEL

The American Kennel Club (AKC), the leading registry of purebred dogs in the United States, first registered an English Springer Spaniel in 1910. The first club that was devoted exclusively to this breed in the United States formed in 1924, named the English Springer

Most spaniels were bred to help their owners hunt. Over time, different breeds were developed for specific purposes. In general, these tasks were divided in to two categories: land and water. In the 19th century, a dog that closely resembles the present-day English Springer Spaniel

The English Springer Spaniel is the oldest of the .... s a hunter and retriever, the English Springer Spani........ rdy hunter and outdoorsman.

Spaniel Field Trial Association. However, the origin and history of the breed goes back much, much further in time.

The English Springer Spaniel's ancestors originated with all other spaniels. As the name "spaniel" implies, these dogs probably came from Spain, as far back as the 15th century. However, it was in Great Britain where the most recent ancestors developed.

developed. As a "springer" it was able to flush, or spring, the game out of hiding into the open for its owner to hunt.

Early in its history, litters would contain larger dogs and smaller dogs. The smaller dogs eventually were no longer bred to the larger dogs because they were employed to hunt different game. The smallerdogs hunted wood cocks, while the larger ones hunted game birds. The smaller dogs became Cocker Spaniels, and the larger dogs became the English Springer Spaniel.

In 1902, The Kennel Club of England was the first purebred dog registry in the world to formally recognize the English Springer Spaniel as a distinct breed. Today, the English Springer Spaniel is well known as an all-around gun dog, specifically of larger game. In addition to its natural desire to help his master hunt, the Springer is a loyal companion, always eager to please.

Throughout the 20th century, both in Great Britain and in the United States, the English Springer Spaniel has developed into an accomplished gun dog in field trials held all year 'round. These field trials lead to a National Championship in both countries. The first of these national championships in the United States was held in 1947.

In addition to doing well in the field, the English Springer Spaniel is no stranger to the dog show ring. In fact, an English Springer Spaniel named Ch. Salilyn's Condor, bred by the famous American breeder Julia Gasow, won Best in Show at the Westminster Kennel Club dog show in 1993. Winning this award at this dog show is the highest honor any dog could ever hope to achieve in its career as a show dog. The equivalent show in England, the Crufts Dog Show has never been won by an English Springer Spaniel.

The English Springer Spaniel has a proud history. Today's Springers are the descendants of these wonderful dogs of the past. They certainly do them proud!

Most at home on the field, the English Springer Spaniel should be permitted to run freely so that he can exercise his limbs. Do, however, keep a watchful eye on him whenever he is outdoors.

Pheasant hunting is popular in both England and the United States. English Springer Spaniels are often chosen to accompany hunters on these outings.

TEMPERAMENT AND PERSONALITY

Your English Springer Spaniel's most prominent personality characteristic is his general love of people and of life. He is a friend to adults and children alike. Even though he is especially patient with children, even the gentlest Springer has his limits!

The Springer is a loyal dog, but his loyalty extends more to the family as a whole, rather than anyone in particular. Do not misunderstand this—-your English Springer Spaniel will follow you to the ends of the earth, but he is more inclined to be a wonderful watchdog for the entire family instead. Strangers are not automatically received with open arms, even with your approval.

His tail always gives him away. Your Springer's tail will tell you all you need to know about his mood. Most of the time, it will be wagging merrily. Above all, the English Springer Spaniel was bred to be a hunting dog, and today's Springer lives up to that calling completely. In the United States and Great Britain especially, his status as a gun dog is well-known. Pheasants are his specialty, but he is known also to hunt for ducks with ease.

Even though the Springer is an outdoor dog, he is at home in the city just as well as in the country.

As countless owners and fanciers can attest, the English Springer Spaniel is one of the most agreeable and patient members of the canine family. Owned and photographed by George Shagawat.

The Springer can tolerate a good deal of rough play with children and will enjoy their attention. It is advisable to always supervise a dog when he is with children.

His size and willingness to please his owners outweigh everything else. If he is to lead a city life, however, he does need regular exercise to keep him happy.

His coat is adapted to be weather resistant. You never have to worry about taking your Springer for a walk in inclement weather. He will probably love it!

The English Springer Spaniel is a very smart dog, and very easy to train. His eagerness to make you happy adds to your ability to train him without much trouble.

Since your Springer puppy will grow up to be a medium-sized dog, he will not require too much of anything. Yet, he will be of substantial size to satisfy those who do not wish to own a small dog. He has a healthy appetite, as well as a healthy attitude. Both at home and in the field, the English Springer Spaniel makes a wonderful companion, either in the country or the city.

STANDARD OF THE ENGLISH SPRINGER SPANIEL

General Appearance and Type: The English Springer Spaniel is a medium-size sporting dog with a neat, compact body and a docked tail. His coat is moderately long and glossy with feathering on his legs, ears, chest and brisket. His doing. At his best, he is endowed with style, symmetry, balance, enthusiasm and is every inch a sporting dog of distinct spaniel character, combining beauty and utility. *To be penalized:* Those lacking true English Springer type in conformation,

Although English Springer puppies appear to be nearly identical, they each develop their own personalities. A breeder can tell you much about the personality of each member of his litter.

pendulous ears, soft gentle expression, sturdy build and friendly wagging tail proclaim him unmistakably a member of the ancient family of spaniels. Taken as a whole, he looks the part of a dog that can go and keep going under difficult hunting conditions, and moreover he enjoys what he is expression, or behavior.

Temperament: The typical Springer is friendly, eager to please, quick to learn, willing to obey. In the show ring, he should exhibit poise, attentiveness, tractability, and should permit himself to be examined by the judge without resentment or cringing.

To be penalized: Excessive timidity, with due allowance for puppies and novice exhibits. But no dog is to receive a ribbon if he behaves in a vicious manner toward handler or judge. Aggressiveness toward other dogs in the ring is not to be construed as viciousness.

Size and Proportion: The Springer is built to cover rough ground with agility and reasonable speed. He should be kept to medium size, neither too small nor too large and heavy to do the work for which he is intended. The ideal shoulder height for dogs is 20 inches; for bitches, 19 inches. Length of topline (the distance from the top of the shoulders to the root of the tail) should be approximately equal to the dog's shoulder height—-never longer than his height—and not appreciably less. The dog too long in body, especially when long in loin, tires easily and lacks the compact outline characteristic of the breed.

Equally undesirable is the dog too short in body for the length of his legs, a condition that destroys his balance and restricts the gait.

Weight is dependent on the dog's other dimensions: a 20-inch dog, well proportioned, in good condition should weigh about 49—55 pounds. The resulting appearance is a well-knit, sturdy dog with good but not too heavy bone, in no way coarse or ponderous.

To be penalized: Over-heavy specimens, cloddy in build. Leggy individuals, too tall for their length and substance. Over-size

The beauty of the English Springer Spaniel's head relies on its refinement; it should be impressive and balanced.

or under-size specimens (those more than one inch under or over the breed ideal).

Color: May be black or liver with white markings or predominately white with black or liver markings; tri-color; black and white or liver and white with tan markings (usually found on eyebrows, cheeks, insides of ears and under tail); blue or liver roan. Any white portions of the coat may be flecked with ticking. All preceding combinations of colors and markings to be equally acceptable.

To be penalized: Off colors such as lemon, red or orange not to place.

Coat: On the ears, chest, legs and belly, the Springer is nicely furnished with a fringe of feathering of moderate length and

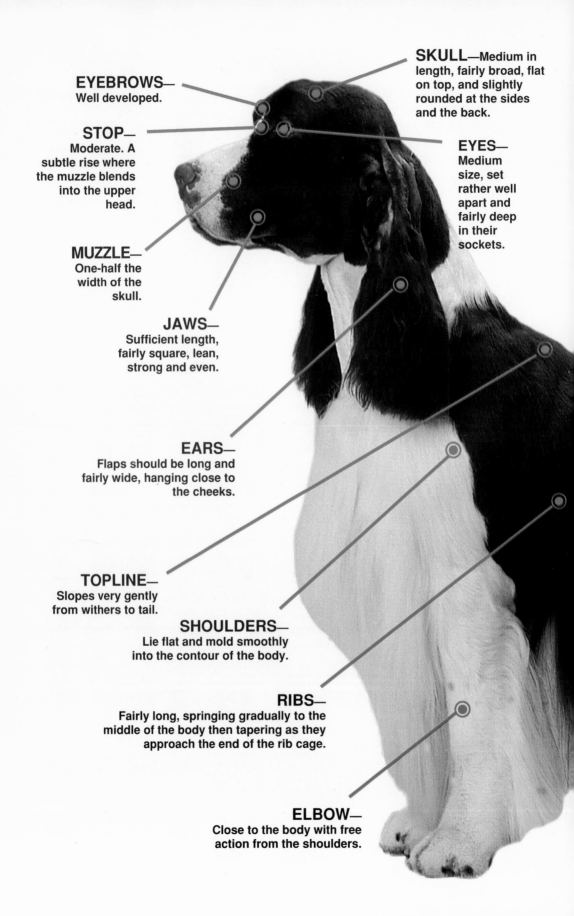

EYEBROWS— Well developed.

STOP— Moderate. A subtle rise where the muzzle blends into the upper head.

MUZZLE— One-half the width of the skull.

JAWS— Sufficient length, fairly square, lean, strong and even.

SKULL—Medium in length, fairly broad, flat on top, and slightly rounded at the sides and the back.

EYES— Medium size, set rather well apart and fairly deep in their sockets.

EARS— Flaps should be long and fairly wide, hanging close to the cheeks.

TOPLINE— Slopes very gently from withers to tail.

SHOULDERS— Lie flat and mold smoothly into the contour of the body.

RIBS— Fairly long, springing gradually to the middle of the body then tapering as they approach the end of the rib cage.

ELBOW— Close to the body with free action from the shoulders.

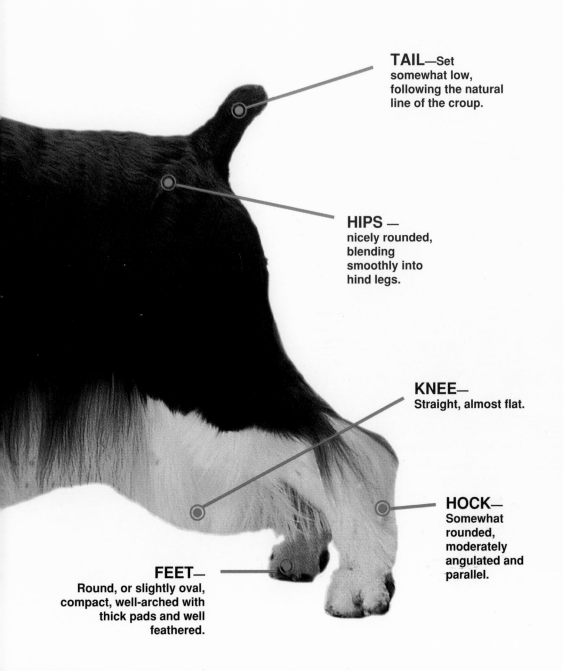

Westminster Kennel Club Best of Breed Winner 1996, Ch. Salilyn's Saturn, owned by Carl Blaine, Fran Sunseri and Julia Gasow.

TAIL—Set somewhat low, following the natural line of the croup.

HIPS — nicely rounded, blending smoothly into hind legs.

KNEE— Straight, almost flat.

HOCK— Somewhat rounded, moderately angulated and parallel.

FEET— Round, or slightly oval, compact, well-arched with thick pads and well feathered.

Your English Springer Spaniel puppy will grow up to closly resemble his ancestors. Be certain to choose your puppy from good, solid stock.

Head: The head is impressive without being heavy. Its beauty lies in a combination of strength and refinement. It is important that the size and proportion be in balance with the rest of the dog. Viewed in profile, the head should appear approximately the same length as the neck and should blend with the body in substance. The skull (upper head) should be of medium length, fairly broad, flat on top, and slightly rounded at the sides and back. The occiput bone inconspicuous, rounded rather than peaked or angular. The foreface (head in front of eyes) approximately the same length as the skull, and in harmony as to width and general character.

Looking down on the head, the muzzle to appear to be about one-

A physically sound Springer will have a balanced, smooth and powerful gait.

heaviness. On the head, front of forelegs, and below hocks on front of hindlegs, the hair is short and fine. The body coat is flat or wavy, of medium length, sufficiently dense to be waterproof, weatherproof and thornproof. The texture should be fine and the hair, clean, glossy, with a live appearance indicative of good health. It is legitimate to trim about the head, feet, and ears to remove dead hair, to thin and shorten excess feathering particularly from the hocks to the feet and elsewhere as required to give a smart, clean appearance.

To be penalized: Rough curly coat. Over-trimming, especially of the body coat. Any chopped, barbered, or artificial effect. Excessive feathering that destroys the clean outline desirable in a sporting dog. Off colors such as lemon, red or orange not to place.

half the width of the skull. As the skull rises from the foreface it makes a brow or "stop," divided by a groove or fluting between the eyes. This groove continues upward and gradually disappears as it reaches the middle of the forehead.

The amount of "stop" can best be described as moderate. It must not be a pronounced feature; rather it is a subtle rise where the muzzle blends into the upper head, further emphasized by the groove and by the position and shape of the eyebrows which should be well-developed. The stop, eyebrow and the chiseling of the bony structure around the eye sockets contribute to the Springer's beautiful and characteristic expression.

Viewed in profile, the topline of the skull and the muzzle lie in two approximately parallel planes. The nasal bone should be straight, with no inclination downward toward the tip of the nose, which gives a down-faced look so undesirable in this breed. Neither should the nasal bone be concave resulting in a "dish-faced" profile; nor convex giving the dog a "Roman nose."

The jaws to be of sufficient length to allow the dog to carry game easily; fairly square, lean, strong, and even (neither undershot nor overshot). The upper lip to come down full and rather square to cover the line of the lower jaw, but lips not to be pendulous nor exaggerated.

The nostrils, well opened and broad, liver color or black depending on the color of the coat. Flesh-colored ("Dudley

Your Springer's back and neck should blend together smoothly, suggesting length and muscularity.

noses") or spotted ("butterfly noses") are undesirable. The cheeks to be flat (not rounded, full, or thick), with nice chiseling under the eyes.

To be penalized: Oval, pointed or heavy skull. Cheeks prominently rounded, thick and protruding. Too much or too little stop. Over-heavy muzzle. Muzzle too short, too thin, too narrow. Pendulous, slobbery lips. Under- or over-shot jaws—a very serious fault, to be heavily penalized.

Teeth: The teeth should be strong, clean, not too small. When the mouth is closed, the teeth should meet in a close scissors bite (the lower incisors touching the inside of the upper incisors).

The English Springer Spaniel's expression is alert, kind and trusting. The eyes of the Springer are the essence of his appeal.

To be penalized: Any deviation from above description. Irregularities due to faulty jaw formation to be severely penalized.

Eyes: More than any other feature, the eyes contribute to the Springer's appeal. Color, placement, and size influence expression and attractiveness. The eyes should be of medium size, neither small, round, full and prominent, nor bold and hard in expression. Set rather well apart and fairly deep in their sockets. The color of the iris to harmonize with the color of the coat, preferably a good dark hazel in liver dogs and black or deep brown in the black and white specimens. The expression should be alert, kindly, trusting. The lids, tight with little or no haw showing.

To be penalized: Eyes yellow or brassy in color or noticeably lighter than the coat. Sharp expression indicating unfriendly or suspicious nature. Loose droopy lids. Prominent haw (the third eyelid or membrane in the inside corner of the eye).

Ears: The correct ear-set is on a level with the line of the eye; on the side of the skull and not too far back. The flaps should be long and fairly wide, hanging close to the cheeks, with no tendency to stand up or out. The leather, thin, approximately long enough to reach the tip of nose.

To be penalized: Short round ears. Ears set too high or too low or too far back on the head.

Neck: The neck should be moderately long, muscular, slightly arched at the crest, and gradually blending into sloping shoulders. Not noticeably upright, nor coming into the body at an abrupt angle.

To be penalized: Short neck, often the sequence to steep shoulders. Concave neck, sometimes called ewe neck or upside-down neck (the opposite of arched). Excessive throatiness.

Body: The body to be well coupled, strong, compact; the chest, deep but not so wide or round as to interfere with the action of the front legs; the brisket, sufficiently developed to reach to the level of the elbows. The ribs, fairly long, springing gradually to the middle of the body then tapering as they approach the end of the rib cage. The back (section between the withers and loin) should be straight and strong, with no tendency to dip or roach. The loins should be strong, short; a slight arch over loins and hip bones. Hips, nicely rounded, blending smoothly into hind legs.

The resulting topline slopes very gently from withers to tail—the line from withers to back descending without a sharp drop; the back practically level; arch over hips somewhat lower than the withers; croup sloping gently to base of tail; tail carried to follow the natural line of the body.

The bottom line, starting on a level with the elbows, to continue backward with almost no up-curve until reaching the end of the ribbed section, then a more noticeable upcurve to the flank, but not enough to make the dog appear small waisted or "tucked up."

The forequarters and hindquarters of your English Springer Spaniel should be equally proportioned and well-muscled for efficient, quick movement.

To be penalized: Body too shallow, indicating lack of brisket. Ribs too flat—sometimes due to immaturity. Ribs too round (barrel-shaped), hampering the gait. Sway-back (dip in back), indicating weakness or lack of muscular development, particularly to be seen when dog is in action and viewed from the side. Roach back (too much arch over loin and extending forward into middle section). Croup falling away too sharply; or croup too high—unsightly faults, detrimental to outline and good movement. Topline sloping sharply, indicating steep withers (straight shoulder placement) and a too low tail-set.

Tail: The Springer's tail is an index both to his temperament and his conformation. Merry tail action is characteristic. The proper set is somewhat low, following the natural line of the croup. The carriage should be nearly horizontal, slightly elevated, when dog is excited. Carried straight up is untypical of the breed. The tail should not be docked too short and should be well fringed with wavy feather. It is legitimate to shape and shorten the feathering but enough should be left to blend with the dog's other furnishings.

To be penalized: Tail habitually upright. Tail set too high or too low. Clamped-down tail (indicating timidity or undependable temperament, even less to be desired than the tail carried too gaily).

Forequarters: Efficient movement in front calls for proper shoulders, the blade sloping back to form an angle with the upper

arm of approximately 90 degrees, which permits the dog to swing his forelegs forward in an easy manner. Shoulders (fairly close together at the tips) to lie flat and mold smoothly into the contour of the body. The forelegs to be straight with the same degree of size to the foot. The bone, strong, slightly flattened, not too heavy or round. The knee, straight, almost flat; the pasterns, short, strong; elbows, close to the body with free action from the shoulders.

To be penalized: Shoulders set at a steep angle limiting the stride. Loaded shoulders (the blades standing out from the body by overdevelopment of the muscles). Loose elbows, crooked legs. Bone too light or too coarse and heavy. Weak pasterns that let down the feet at a pronounced angle.

Hindquarters: The Springer should be shown in hard muscular condition, well developed in hips and thighs and the whole rear assembly should suggest strength and driving power. The hip joints to be set rather wide apart and the hips nicely rounded. The thighs broad and muscular; the stifle joint strong and moderately bent. The hock somewhat rounded, not small and sharp in contour, and moderately angulated. Leg from hock joint to foot pad, short and strong with good bone structure. When viewed from the rear, the hocks should be parallel whether the dog is standing or in motion.

To be penalized: Too little or too much angulation. Narrow, undeveloped thighs. Hocks too

It is hard to predict what your Springer puppy will be like as an adult, but if he has healthy and well adjusted parents, he is off to a good start. Remember when comparing your Springer against the standard, no dog is perfect.

The English Springer Spaniel is every inch a sporting dog of distinct spaniel character, combining beauty and utility.

short or too long (a proportion of one-third the distance from hip joint to foot is ideal). Flabby muscles. Weakness of joints.

Feet: The feet should be round, or slightly oval, compact, well arched, medium sized with thick pads, well feathered between the toes. Excess hair to be removed to show the natural shape and size of the foot.

To be penalized: Thin, open, or splayed feet (flat with spreading toes). Hare foot (long, rather narrow foot).

Movement: In judging the Springer there should be emphasis on proper movement, which is the final test of a dog's conformation and soundness. Prerequisite to good movement is balance of the front and rear assemblies. The two must match in angulation and muscular development if the gait is to be smooth and effortless.

Good shoulders laid back at an angle that permits a long stride are just as essential as the excellent rear quarters that provide the driving power.

When viewed from the front, the dog's legs should appear to swing forward in a free and easy manner, with no tendency for the feet to cross over or interfere with each other. Viewed from the rear, the hocks should reach well under the body following on a line with the forelegs, the rear legs parallel, neither too widely nor too closely spaced.

As speed increases, there is a natural tendency for the legs to converge toward the center line of gravity or a single line of travel.

Two of the acceptable coat colors of the English Springer Spaniel—black and white and liver and white.

Seen from the side, the Springer should exhibit a good long forward stride, without high-stepping or wasted motion.

To be penalized*:* Short choppy stride, mincing steps with up and down movement, hopping. Moving with forefeet wide, giving roll or swing to body. Weaving or crossing of forefeet or hind feet. Cowhocks—hocks turning in toward each other.

In judging the English Springer Spaniel, the overall picture is a primary consideration. It is urged that the judge look for type which includes general appearance, outline, temperament and soundness, especially as seen when the dog is in motion.

Inasmuch as the dog with a smooth easy gait must be reasonably sound and well balanced, he is to be highly regarded in the show ring; however, not to the extent of pardoning him for not looking like an English Springer Spaniel. A quite untypical dog, leggy, foreign in head and expression, may move well, but he should not be placed over a good all-around specimen that has a minor fault in movement. It should be remembered that the English Springer Spaniel is first and foremost a sporting dog of the spaniel family and he must look and behave and move in character.

YOUR NEW ENGLISH SPRINGER SPANIEL PUPPY

SELECTION

When you do pick out a English Springer Spaniel puppy as a pet, don't be hasty; the longer you study puppies, the better you will understand them. Make it your transcendent concern to select only one that radiates good health and spirit and is lively on his feet, whose eyes are bright, whose coat shines, and who comes forward eagerly to make and to cultivate your acquaintance. Don't fall for any shy little darling that wants to retreat to his bed or his box, or plays coy behind other puppies or people, or hides his head under your arm or jacket appealing to your protective instinct. *Pick the English Springer Spaniel puppy who forthrightly picks you! The feeling of attraction should be mutual!*

DOCUMENTS

Now, a little paper work is in order. When you purchase a purebred English Springer Spaniel puppy, you should receive a transfer of ownership, registration material, and other "papers" (a list of the immunization shots, if any, the puppy may have been given; a

Personalities vary within a litter of puppies, so choose one that will fit your lifestyle.

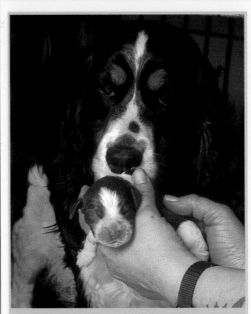

Puppies should be handled by no one other than the breeder until they have received their first set of shots. The newborns' immune systems are not yet built up and it is easy for them to fall ill.

note on whether or not the puppy has been wormed; a diet and feeding schedule to which the puppy is accustomed) and you are welcomed as a fellow owner to a long, pleasant association with a most lovable pet, and more (news)paper work.

GENERAL PREPARATION

You have chosen to own a particular English Springer Spaniel puppy. You have chosen it very carefully over all other breeds and all other puppies. So before you ever get that English Springer Spaniel puppy home, you will have prepared for its arrival by reading everything you can get your hands on having to do with the management of English Springer Spaniels and puppies. True, you will run into

many conflicting opinions, but at least you will not be starting "blind." Read, study, digest. Talk over your plans with your veterinarian, other "English Springer Spaniel people," and the seller of your English Springer Spaniel puppy.

When you get your English Springer Spaniel puppy, you will find that your reading and study are far from finished. You've just scratched the surface in your plan to provide the greatest possible comfort and health for your English Springer Spaniel; and, by the same token, you do want to assure yourself of the greatest possible enjoyment of this wonderful creature. You must be ready for this puppy mentally as well as in the physical requirements.

TRANSPORTATION

If you take the puppy home by car, protect him from drafts, particularly in cold weather. Wrapped in a towel and carried in the arms or lap of a passenger, the English Springer Spaniel puppy will usually make the trip without mishap. If the pup starts to drool and to squirm, stop the car for a few minutes. Have newspapers handy in case of car-sickness. A covered carton lined with newspapers provides protection for puppy and car, if you are driving alone. Avoid excitement and unnecessary handling of the puppy on arrival. A English Springer Spaniel puppy is a very small "package" to be making a complete change of surroundings and company, and he needs frequent rest and refreshment to renew his vitality.

THE FIRST DAY AND NIGHT

When your English Springer Spaniel puppy arrives in your home, put him down on the floor and don't pick him up again, except when it is absolutely necessary. He is a dog, a real dog, and must not be lugged around like a rag doll. Handle him as little as possible, and permit no one to pick him up and baby him. To repeat, *put your English Springer Spaniel puppy on the floor or the ground and let him stay there except when it may be necessary to do otherwise.*

Quite possibly your English Springer Spaniel puppy will be afraid for a while in his new surroundings, without his mother and littermates. Comfort him and reassure him, but don't console him. Don't give him the "oh-you-

Choose a puppy that is alert and active, with bright eyes and a shiny coat.

poor-itsy-bitsy-puppy" treatment. Be calm, friendly, and reassuring. Encourage him to walk around and sniff over his new home. If it's dark, put on the lights. Let him

Its hard to resist these adorable English Springer Spaniel puppies, but make sure that your decision to bring one home is a carefully considered one.

Reputable breeders start their puppies on the road to good nutrition, so stick with your pup's original diet when you first bring him home. Be certain to make any changes gradually.

roam for a few minutes while you and everyone else concerned sit quietly or go about your routine business. Let the puppy come back to you.

Playmates may cause an immediate problem if the new English Springer Spaniel puppy is to be greeted by children or other pets. If not, you can skip this subject. The natural affinity between puppies and children calls for some supervision until a live-and-let-live relationship is established. This applies particularly to a Christmas puppy, when there is more excitement than usual and more chance for a puppy to swallow

something upsetting. It is a better plan to welcome the puppy several days before or after the holiday week. Like a baby, your English Springer Spaniel puppy needs much rest and should not be over-handled. Once a child realizes that a puppy has "feelings" similar to his own, and can readily be hurt or injured, the opportunities for play and responsibilities provide exercise and training for both.

For his first night with you, he should be put where he is to sleep every night—say in the kitchen, since its floor can usually be easily cleaned. Let him explore the kitchen to his heart's content;

close doors to confine him there. Prepare his food and feed him lightly the first night. Give him a pan with some water in it—not a lot, since most puppies will try to drink the whole pan dry. Give him an old coat or shirt to lie on. Since a coat or shirt will be strong in human scent, he will pick it out to lie on, thus furthering his feeling of security in the room where he has just been fed.

HOUSEBREAKING HELPS

Now, sooner or later—mostly sooner—your new English Springer Spaniel puppy is going to "puddle" on the floor. First take a newspaper and lay it on the puddle until the urine is soaked

Take your puppy outdoors to eliminate immediately after waking and after eating. Do not allow your puppy back in the house until he has done his "business." Remember to praise him lavishly when he is finished.

Housebreaking is the first training lesson your English Springer Spaniel puppy will learn. This is something that must be learned for your puppy's well-being, as well as your own.

up onto the paper. *Save this paper.* Now take a cloth with soap and water, wipe up the floor and dry it well. Then take the wet paper and place it on a fairly large square of newspapers in a convenient corner. When cleaning up, always keep a piece of wet paper on top of the others. Every time he wants to "squat," he will seek out this spot and use the papers. (This routine is rarely necessary for more than three days.) Now leave your English Springer Spaniel puppy for the night. Quite probably he will cry and howl a bit; some are more stubborn than others on this matter. But let him stay alone for the night. This may seem harsh treatment, but it is the best procedure in the long run. Just let him cry; he will weary of it sooner or later.

FEEDING YOUR ENGLISH SPRINGER SPANIEL

Now let's talk about feeding your English Springer Spaniel, a subject so simple that it's amazing there is so much nonsense and misunderstanding about it. Is it expensive to feed a English Springer Spaniel? No, it is not! You can feed your English Springer Spaniel economically and keep him in perfect shape the year round, or you can feed him expensively. He'll (and possibly turn them into poor, "picky" eaters) they will eat almost anything that they become accustomed to. Many dogs flatly refuse to eat nice, fresh beef. They pick around it and eat everything else. But meat—bah! Why? They aren't accustomed to it! They'd eat rabbit fast enough, but they refuse beef because they aren't used to it.

Puppies receive their first nourishment from their mother. By the time they are ready to go home they should be eating a nutritionally sound dog food.

thrive either way, and let's see why this is true.

First of all, remember a English Springer Spaniel is a dog. Dogs do not have a high degree of selectivity in their food, and unless you spoil them with great variety

VARIETY NOT NECESSARY

A good general rule of thumb is forget all human preferences and don't give a thought to variety. Choose the right diet for your English Springer Spaniel and feed it to him day after day, year after year, winter and summer. But what is the right diet?

Hundreds of thousands of dollars have been spent in canine nutrition research. The results are pretty conclusive, so you needn't go into a lot of experimenting with trials of this and that every other week. Research has proven just what your dog needs to eat and to keep healthy.

DOG FOOD

There are almost as many right diets as there are dog experts, but the basic diet most often recommended is one that consists of a dry food, either meal or kibble form. There are several of excellent quality, manufactured by reliable companies, research tested, and nationally advertised. They are inexpensive, highly satisfactory, and easily available in stores everywhere in containers

A complete and nutritionally balanced diet will be evident in your English Springer Spaniel's shiny coat and overall healthy appearance.

Springer Spaniels love "people food," but must learn to never just help themselves! Good manners is a necessary quality in your dog.

of five to 50 pounds. Larger amounts cost less per pound, usually.

If you have a choice of brands, it is usually safer to choose the better known one; but even so, carefully read the analysis on the package. Do not choose any food in which the protein level is less than 25 percent, and be sure that this protein comes from both animal and vegetable sources. The good dog foods have meat meal, fish meal, liver, and such, plus protein from alfalfa and soy beans, as well as some dried-milk product. Note the vitamin content carefully. See that they are all there in good proportions; and be especially certain that the food contains properly high levels of vitamins A and D, two of the most

Puppies need to chew as part of their physical and mental development. Give your puppies something safe and fun, like a Nylabone® to gnaw on!

Raising your English Springer Spaniel's food and water dishes and giving him two meals a day will reduce his tendency to gulp down his food and lessen his chances of bloat.

perishable and important ones. Note the B-complex level, but don't worry about carbohydrate and mineral levels. These substances are plentiful and cheap and not likely to be lacking in a good brand.

The advice given for how to choose a dry food also applies to moist or canned types of dog foods, if you decide to feed one of these.

Having chosen a really good food, feed it to your English Springer Spaniel as the manufacturer directs. And once you've started, stick to it. Never change if you can possibly help it. A switch from one meal or kibble-type food can usually be made without too much upset; however, a change will almost invariably give you (and your English Springer Spaniel) some trouble.

Your English Springer Spaniel will be happier and his teeth will be healthier if you give him a giant-sized POPpup™ to chew on. Every POPpup™ is 100% edible and enhanced with dog-friendly ingredients like liver, cheese, spinach, chicken, carrots or potatoes.

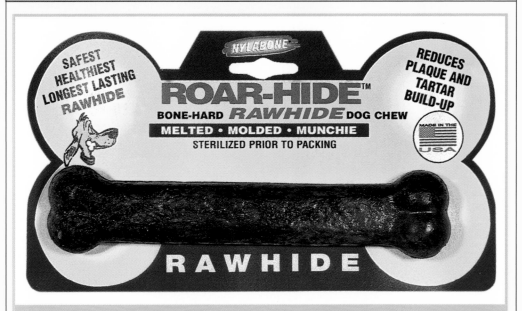

To combat boredom and relieve your English Springer Spaniel's natural desire to chew, there's nothing better than a Roar-Hide™. Unlike common Rawhide, this bone won't turn into a gooey mess when chewed on, so your dog won't choke on small pieces of it. The Roarhide™ is completely edible, high in protein and low in fat.

WHEN SUPPLEMENTS ARE NEEDED

Now what about supplements of various kinds, mineral and vitamin, or the various oils? They are all okay to add to your English Springer Spaniel's food. However, if you are feeding your English Springer Spaniel a correct diet, and this is easy to do, no supplements are necessary unless your English Springer Spaniel has been improperly fed, has been sick, or is having puppies. Vitamins and minerals are naturally present in all the foods; and to ensure against any loss through processing, they are added in concentrated form to the dog food you use. Except on the advice of your veterinarian, added amounts of vitamins can prove harmful to your English Springer Spaniel! The same risk goes with minerals.

The Nylabone® company makes many toys that your English Springer Spaniel will be happy to play with. This Springer is having a great time with his owner and the Nylabone® Tug Toy.

The English Springer's ears are so long and wide that they get in his way while eating. These two Springers have their ears tucked into scarves so that they can eat in comfort.

FEEDING SCHEDULE

When and how much food to give your English Springer Spaniel? Most dogs do better if fed two or three smaller meals per day—this is not only better but vital to larger and deep-chested dogs. As to how to prepare the food and how much to give, it is generally best to follow the directions on the food package. Your own English Springer Spaniel may want a little more or a little less.

Fresh, cool water should always be available to your English Springer Spaniel. This is important to good health throughout his lifetime.

ALL ENGLISH SPRINGER SPANIELS NEED TO CHEW

Puppies and young English Springer Spaniels need something with resistance to chew on while their teeth and jaws are developing—for cutting the puppy teeth, to induce growth of the permanent teeth under the puppy teeth, to assist in getting rid of the puppy teeth at the proper time, to help the permanent teeth through the gums, to ensure normal jaw development, and to settle the permanent teeth solidly in the jaws.

The adult English Springer Spaniel's desire to chew stems from the instinct for tooth

Fresh water should be available for your dog at all times—when he is inside or out. Outdoor dogs will appreciate a bowl left where they can come to drink when thirsty.

A Gumabone® Frisbee™* is a great toy for games of fetch with your English Springer Spaniel. It is flexible enough for your dog to carry, and the bone on top makes it easy to pick up. *The trademark Frisbee is used under license from Mattel, Inc., CA, USA.

The Tug-Toy from Nylabone® is a flavorful device that can be enjoyed by both English Springer Spaniel and owner.

cleaning, gum massage, and jaw exercise—plus the need for an outlet for periodic doggie tensions.

This is why dogs, especially puppies and young dogs, will often destroy property worth hundreds of dollars when their chewing instinct is not diverted from their owner's possessions. And this is why you should provide your English Springer Spaniel with something to chew—something that has the necessary functional qualities, is desirable from the English Springer Spaniel's viewpoint, and is safe for him.

It is very important that your English Springer Spaniel not be permitted to chew on anything he can break or on any indigestible thing from which he can bite sizable chunks. Sharp pieces, such as from a bone which can be broken by a dog, may pierce the intestinal wall and kill. Indigestible things that can be bitten off in chunks, such as from shoes or rubber or plastic toys, may cause an intestinal stoppage (if not regurgitated) and bring painful death, unless surgery is promptly performed.

Strong natural bones, such as 4- to 8-inch lengths of round shin bone from mature beef—either the kind you can get from a butcher or one of the variety available commercially in pet stores—may serve your English Springer Spaniel's teething needs if his mouth is large enough to handle them effectively. You may be tempted to give your English Springer Spaniel puppy a smaller bone and he may not be able to break it when you do, but puppies grow rapidly and the power of their jaws constantly increases until maturity. This means that a growing English Springer Spaniel may break one of the smaller bones at any time, swallow the pieces, and die painfully before you realize what is wrong.

All hard natural bones are very abrasive. If your English Springer Spaniel is an avid chewer, natural bones may wear away his teeth prematurely; hence, they then should be taken away from your dog when the teething purposes have been served. The badly worn, and usually painful, teeth of many mature dogs can be traced to excessive chewing on natural bones.

Your English Springer Spaniel needs a chew device that's up to his standard, and with the Hercules® bone, he's got one. The unique design of the Hercules enables aggressive chewers to grab onto it anywhere for a solid, satisfying chew.

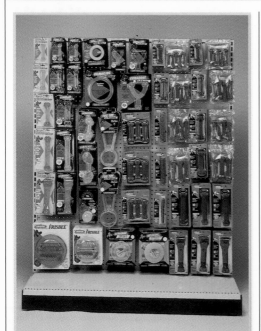

Most pet shops have complete walls dedicated to safe pacifiers.

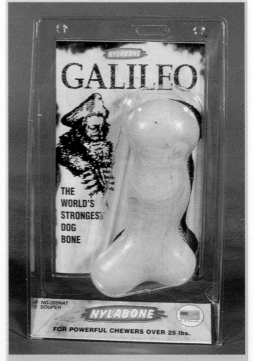

The Galileo™ is an extremely tough nylon pacifier. Its design is based upon original sketches by Galileo. A book explaining the history and workings of the design comes inside each package. This might well be the best design for an English Springer Spaniel.

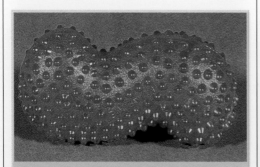

Some Springers are strong chewers and they require strong chew devices. The Hercules® is a dental device that is made from very heavy polyurethane.

Raised dental tips on each dog bone work wonders with controlling plaque in a Springer's teeth.

Use only a large size Nylabone® for your English Springer Spaniel.

Contrary to popular belief, knuckle bones that can be chewed up and swallowed by your English Springer Spaniel provide little, if any, usable calcium or other nutriment. They do, however, disturb the digestion of most dogs and cause them to vomit the nourishing food they need.

Dried rawhide products of various types, shapes, sizes, and prices are available on the market and have become quite popular. However, they don't serve the primary chewing functions very well; they are a bit messy when wet from mouthing, and most English Springer Spaniels chew them up rather rapidly—but they have been considered safe for dogs until recently. Now, more and more incidents of death, and near death, by strangulation have been reported to be the results of partially swallowed chunks of rawhide swelling in the throat. More recently, some veterinarians have been attributing cases of acute constipation to large pieces of incompletely digested rawhide in the intestine.

A new product, molded rawhide, is very safe. During the process, the rawhide is melted and then injection molded into the familiar dog shape. It is very hard and is eagerly accepted by English Springer Spaniels. The melting process also sterilizes the rawhide. Don't confuse this with pressed rawhide, which is nothing more than small strips of rawhide squeezed together.

The nylon bones, especially those with natural meat and bone

The Nylabone/Gumabone® Pooch Pacifier enables your English Springer Spaniel to slowly chew off the knobs while they clean their own teeth. The knobs develop elastic frays that act as a toothbrush. These pacifiers are extremely effective as detailed scientific studies have shown.

fractions added, are probably the most complete, safe, and economical answer to the chewing need. Dogs cannot break them or bite off sizable chunks; hence, they are completely safe—and being longer lasting than other things offered for the purpose, they are economical.

Hard chewing raises little bristle-like projections on the surface of the nylon bones—to provide effective interim tooth cleaning and vigorous gum massage, much in the same way your toothbrush does it for you. The little projections are raked off and swallowed in the form of thin shavings, but the chemistry of the nylon is such that they break down in the stomach fluids and pass through without effect.

The toughness of the nylon provides the strong chewing resistance needed for important jaw exercise and effectively aids teething functions, but there is no tooth wear because nylon is non-abrasive. Being inert, nylon does not support the growth of microorganisms; and it can be washed in soap and water or it can be sterilized by boiling or in an autoclave.

Nylabone® is highly recommended by veterinarians as a safe, healthy nylon bone that can't splinter or chip. Nylabone® is frizzled by the dog's chewing action, creating a toothbrush-like surface that cleanses the teeth and massages the gums. Nylabone® is superior to the cheaper bones because it is made of virgin nylon, which is the strongest and longest-lasting type of nylon available. The cheaper bones are made from recycled or re-ground nylon scraps, and have a tendency to break apart and split easily.

Nothing, however, substitutes for periodic professional attention for your English Springer Spaniel's teeth and gums, not any more than your toothbrush can do that for you. Have your English Springer Spaniel's teeth cleaned at least once a year by your veterinarian (twice a year is better) and he will be happier, healthier, and far more pleasant to live with.

The Nylabone® company makes a variety of chew toys that will be enjoyed by your English Springer Spaniel. Available in an array of sizes and colors, you will be sure to find one suitable for your Springer friend!

GROOMING YOUR ENGLISH SPRINGER SPANIEL

The English Springer Spaniel does not need as much care as some other dogs, but there are a few things that you should keep in mind. It's a good idea to start your grooming session with a quick check of your dog's eyes and teeth. Simply check to see if your Springer's eyes are free of redness and any abnormal discharge. Check your dog's teeth to see if they are covered with tartar. Brushing your dog's teeth regularly should reduce and prevent tartar buildup. Make sure to use toothpaste specially designed for dogs. Human toothpaste will upset your dog's stomach and possibly harm your dog's tooth enamel.

After checking his eyes and teeth, it's time to pay attention to your English Springer Spaniel's coat and nails. Even if your young Springer puppy gets dirty, you should not bathe him until he is at least three months old. This means that you will have to be extra careful about combing and brushing his coat on a regular basis, preferably every day.

Start grooming your English Springer Spaniel by letting him stand or lie down on a non-skid table and brushing his coat with a soft-bristle brush.

When you bathe your Springer Spaniel, make sure to rinse his coat thoroughly. Excess shampoo can cause skin irritation.

Combing and brushing your dog regularly will let you bathe your dog less frequently. In addition, regular combing and brushing are better for him than frequent bathing. Your Springer's coat is naturally weather resistant. Frequent bathing, over time, can strip his coat of the natural oils that make his coat weather resistant. Yet, this is not to say that you should live with a dirty dog! If he's dirty, smelly, or just "a bit grubby," give him a bath!

You will need a good steel comb and a stiff brush to groom your Springer's coat properly. Comb and brush him at least three or four times a week to keep his coat's natural oils evenly distributed, and to prevent

You would be surprised at how much food and dirt can accumulate on a Springer puppy's coat, especially the ears. Since his ears are long, they will inevitably hang into the food and water dishes. This will still be a concern even when your puppy is full grown. Even if your Springer is full grown and he doesn't need a bath just yet, it's still a good idea to clean his ears regularly.

As with most other dogs, the English Springer Spaniel only needs to be bathed when he is dirty or smelly. However, if your dog is a show dog, he will need to be bathed before each competition. Make sure to use special dog shampoos for regular bathing. These can be found at most pet supply shops.

Following a regular grooming regimen is an excellent way to detect any health problems, as well as a great way to spend relaxing quality time with your dog.

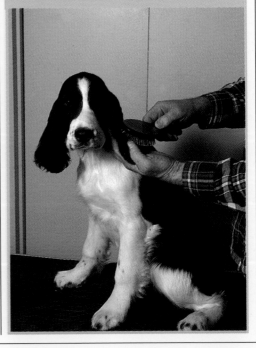

Because your Springer's ears are long and pendulous it is important that you thoroughly check them for burrs and other foreign objects during the grooming process.

Your English Springer's ears require extra care because they are long and droopy. This Springer's ears are wrapped so that the hair is not too full or fluffy.

clean, you should pay very careful attention to keeping the inside of his ears clean as well. Ear mites love the damp, dark and warm inside ear. Check them two or three times a week. If you smell an unusual odor or notice that your dog is holding or shaking its head on one side, consult your veterinarian. Wrapping a cloth around your finger and wiping the inside ear carefully with either alcohol or mineral oil should be enough to keep it clean. Do not put your fingers into the inner ear when cleaning your dog's ears.

You may want to trim some hair from around your Springer's ears to help prevent ear mites and other ear trouble.

A thorough examination of your English Springer Spaniel's mouth, teeth and gums should be part of his grooming regimen.

dandruff in his coat. An area that may need special attention is where the outer ears meet the top of his head. Here the hair is prone to developing mats, so use a fine tooth comb to prevent these from forming.

A dog that is fed the proper oils in his regular diet will most surely have a great-looking coat. Most dog foods already provide for the proper balance. However, if you think your Springer's coat looks flat or dry, you may want to add some cod-liver oil to his diet. Do not use vegetable fats. Consult your veterinarian for more detailed advice if you choose to supplement or change your dog's diet.

In addition to keeping the outside of your Springer's ears

Another place you may want to trim some hair on a regular basis is around his toes, especially in the winter. This will prevent your dog from collecting dangerous salts and other chemicals used on pavements to prevent icing. Regular trimming of hair around the toes also adds to your Springer's neat appearance.

Trim your dog's nails on a regular basis as well as his hair around his toes. Your Springer puppy's toenails will grow quickly and curl underneath his paw pads. This could be painful and even harmful. Clip the ends of each toenail with a special dog nail clipper, available at most pet-supply stores.

Make sure to not cut too far down the toenail, especially if your Springer has dark toenails. Cutting too much will result in cutting the quick, which is the fleshy part of the nail. In turn, this will cause bleeding, and be very painful. The bleeding can be stopped with a styptic pencil (so have one on hand!).

Your English Springer Spaniel will certainly appreciate the attention and the benefits that regular grooming will provide for him. To make sure this is so, get your puppy used to being handled from the first day he becomes part of your life. By doing this, and making it fun instead of a chore, you will always have a dog that is ready and willing to be groomed.

Pretty as a picture. The English Springer Spaniel has a long and lustrous coat that requires constant care.

It must be remembered that the English Springer Spaniel is first and foremost a sporting dog, and this should always be reflected in his conformation and temperament.

TRAINING YOUR ENGLISH SPRINGER SPANIEL

You owe proper training to your English Springer Spaniel. The right and privilege of being trained is his birthright; and whether your English Springer Spaniel is going to be a handsome, well-mannered housedog and companion, a show dog, or whatever possible use he may be put to, the basic training is always the same—all must start with basic obedience, or what might be called "manner training."

Your English Springer Spaniel must come instantly when called and obey the "Sit" or "Down" command just as fast; he must walk quietly at "Heel," whether on or off lead. He must be mannerly and polite wherever he goes; he must be polite to strangers on the street and in stores. He must be mannerly in the presence of other dogs. He must not bark at children on roller skates, motorcycles, or other domestic animals. And he must be restrained from chasing cats. It is not a dog's inalienable right to chase cats, and he must be reprimanded for it.

Keep your English Springer Spaniel on lead while practicing training techniques outdoors.

PROFESSIONAL TRAINING

How do you go about this training? Well, it's a very simple procedure, pretty well standardized by now. First, if you can afford the extra expense, you may send your English Springer Spaniel to a professional trainer, where in 30 to 60 days he will learn how to be a "good dog." If you enlist the services of a good professional trainer, follow his advice of when to come to see the dog. No, he won't forget you, but too-frequent visits at the wrong time may slow down his training progress. And using a "pro" trainer means that you will have to go for some training, too, after the trainer feels your English Springer Spaniel is ready to go

Use your dog's name when giving him a command and be sure to establish good eye contact.

to you and also tell you when and how to correct your English Springer Spaniel's errors. Then, too, working with such a group, your English Springer Spaniel will learn to get along with other dogs. And, what is more important, he will learn to do exactly what he is told to do, no matter how much confusion there is around him or how great the temptation is to go his own way.

Write to your national kennel club for the location of a training club or class in your locality. Sign up. Go to it regularly—every session! Go early and leave late! Both you and your English Springer Spaniel will benefit tremendously.

Crates make housetraining your pet much easier, because dogs do not want to soil where they eat and sleep.

home. You will have to learn how your English Springer Spaniel works, just what to expect of him and how to use what the dog has learned after he is home.

OBEDIENCE TRAINING CLASS

Another way to train your English Springer Spaniel (many experienced English Springer Spaniel people think this is the best) is to join an obedience training class right in your own community. There is such a group in nearly every community nowadays. Here you will be working with a group of people who are also just starting out. You will actually be training your own dog, since all work is done under the direction of a head trainer who will make suggestions

Agility is just one of the many activities in which English Springer Spaniels can demonstrate their athletic and competitive prowess.

TRAIN HIM BY THE BOOK

The third way of training your English Springer Spaniel is by the book. Yes, you can do it this way and do a good job of it too. But in using the book method, select a book, buy it, study it carefully; then study it some more, until the procedures are almost second nature to you. Then start your training. But stay with the book and its advice and exercises. Don't start in and then make up a few rules of your own. If you don't follow the book, you'll get into jams you can't get out of by yourself. If after a few hours of short training sessions your English Springer Spaniel is still not working as he should, get back to the book for a study session, because it's your fault, not the dog's! The procedures of dog training have been so well systemized that it must be your fault, since literally thousands of fine English Springer Spaniels have been trained by the book.

After your English Springer Spaniel is "letter perfect" under all conditions, then, if you wish, go on to advanced training and trick work.

Your English Springer Spaniel will love his obedience training, and you'll burst with pride at the finished product! Your English Springer Spaniel will enjoy life even more, and you'll enjoy your English Springer Spaniel more. And remember—you *owe good training to your English Springer Spaniel.*

SHOWING YOUR ENGLISH SPRINGER SPANIEL

A show English Springer Spaniel is a comparatively rare thing. He is one out of several litters of puppies. He happens to be born with a degree of physical perfection that closely approximates the standard by which the breed is judged in the show ring. Such a dog should, on maturity, be able to win or approach his championship in good, fast company at the larger shows. Upon finishing his championship, he is apt to be as highly desirable as a breeding animal. As a proven stud, he will automatically command a high price for service.

Showing English Springer Spaniels is a lot of fun—yes, but it is a highly competitive sport. While all the experts were once beginners, the odds are against a novice. You will be showing against experienced handlers, often people who have devoted a lifetime to breeding, picking the right ones, and then showing those dogs through to their championships. Moreover, the most perfect English Springer Spaniel ever born has faults, and in your hands the faults will be far more evident than with the experienced handler who knows how to minimize his English

Conformation shows evaluate dogs against the breed standard. The breeder of your puppy or another experienced breeder is a good source for evaluating your puppy for show potential.

Showing your English Springer Spaniel takes time, dedication and teamwork, but you and your dog can only benefit from the bond that will form between you.

your English Springer Spaniel is approaching maturity, start out at match shows, and, with this experience for both of you, then go gunning for the big wins at the big shows.

Next step, read the standard by which the English Springer Spaniel is judged. Study it until you know it by heart. Having done this, and while your puppy is at home (where he should be) growing into a normal, healthy English Springer Spaniel, go to every dog show you can possibly reach. Sit at the ringside and watch English Springer Spaniel judging. Keep your ears and eyes open. Do your own judging,

The "heel" command is a basic command that every dog should learn. In the show ring, it is very important that your English Springer not pull or tug away from the handler.

Springer Spaniel's faults. These are but a few points on the sad side of the picture.

The experienced handler, as I say, was not born knowing the ropes. He learned—*and so can you!* You can if you will put in the same time, study and keen observation that he did. But it will take time!

KEY TO SUCCESS

First, search for a truly fine show prospect. Take the puppy home, raise him by the book, and as carefully as you know how, give him every chance to mature into the English Springer Spaniel you hoped for. My advice is to keep your dog out of big shows, even Puppy Classes, until he is mature. Maturity in the male is roughly two years; with the female, 14 months or so. When

Junior handling is a wonderful way for a young person to build confidence and a strong foundation for successful future showing and handling.

against the standard. In "ringside judging," forget your personal preference for this or that feature. What does the standard say about it? Watch carefully as the judge places the dogs in a given class. It is difficult from the ringside always to see why number one was placed over the second dog. Try to follow the judge's reasoning. Later try to talk with the judge after he is finished. Ask him questions as to why he placed certain English Springer Spaniels and not others. Listen while the judge explains his placings, and, I'll say right here, any judge worthy of his license should be able to give reasons.

When you're not at the ringside, talk with the fanciers and breeders who have English

holding each of those dogs against the standard, which you now know by heart.

In your evaluations, don't start looking for faults. Look for the virtues—the best qualities. How does a given English Springer Spaniel shape up against the standard? Having looked for and noted the virtues, then note the faults and see what prevents a given English Springer Spaniel from standing correctly or moving well. Weigh these faults against the virtues, since, ideally, every feature of the dog should contribute to the harmonious whole dog.

"RINGSIDE JUDGING"

It's a good practice to make notes on each English Springer Spaniel, always holding the dog

Handlers must wear comfortable, practical clothing that does not distract attention from the dog they are showing.

Springer Spaniels. Don't be afraid to ask opinions or say that you don't know. You have a lot of listening to do, and it will help you a great deal and speed up your personal progress if you are a good listener.

THE NATIONAL CLUB

You will find it worthwhile to join the national English Springer Spaniel club and to subscribe to its magazine. From the national club, you will learn the location of an approved regional club near you. Now, when your young English Springer Spaniel is eight to ten months old, find out the dates of match shows in your section of the country. These differ from regular shows only in that no championship points are given. These shows are especially designed to launch young dogs (and new handlers) on a show career.

ENTER MATCH SHOWS

With the ring deportment you have watched at big shows firmly in mind and practice, enter your English Springer Spaniel in as many match shows as you can. When in the ring, you have two jobs. One is to see to it that your English Springer Spaniel is always being seen to its best advantage. The other job is to keep your eye on the judge to see what he may want you to do next. Watch only the judge and your English Springer Spaniel. Be quick and be alert; do exactly as the judge directs. Don't speak to him except to answer his questions. If he does something you don't like, don't say so. And don't irritate the judge (and everybody else) by constantly talking and fussing with your dog.

In moving about the ring, remember to keep clear of dogs beside you or in front of you. It is my advice to you *not* to show your English Springer Spaniel in a regular point show until he is at least close to maturity and after both you and your dog have had time to perfect ring manners and poise in the match shows.

Handlers must pose their show dogs in the most flattering position to emphasize the dog's specific strengths and hide any flaws.

Successful showing requires dedication and preparation, but most of all, it should be an enjoyable experience for handlers and dogs alike.

HEALTH OF YOUR SPRINGER

Your English Springer Spaniel's continued good health will depend on many factors. Heredity and your dog's environment both contribute to the overall health of your Springer. One of the most important factors in maintaining your dog's health is your veterinarian. Picking the right veterinarian will be one of the

Word of mouth is still one of the most reliable methods of finding a veterinarian. Even if you just want to go to the closest vet clinic to your home, or pick one out of the local business directory, make sure to ask the veterinarian questions about his or her policies, practice, etc. If you do not feel comfortable with the

Find out which vaccinations your puppy has received prior to bringing him home, for his health as well as the health of your family.

most important decisions you make on behalf of your Springer.

How do you go about picking a veterinarian? Ask your friends and neighbors about their veterinarian and how satisfied they are with his or her services.

veterinarian or cannot hold a reasonable conversation this him or her, pick another one!

Under no circumstances should you try to be your own veterinarian. Your vet should be the first person you call when your dog is sick or an accident occurs. Of course, as with humans, your dog may need first aid after an accident. In this case, it is advisable to have a dog first aid kit available. The contents of the dog first aid kit should include tweezers, scissors, tape, bandages, a thermometer, surgical scissors, cotton, petroleum jelly, enema equipment, antiseptic power and a styptic pencil. Consult your veterinarian for additional dog first-aid kit suggestions.

When should you call your veterinarian? Whenever you have any doubt as to your dog's well-being. You are with your dog the most. You know when he is feeling well and behaving in a normal manner. If he acts otherwise, you should monitor him closely for other signs.

Your veterinarian will check your English Springer from head to toe. Your dog's eyes should be dark and clear, without any signs of redness or irritation.

Annual vaccinations are necessary to keep your English Springer Spaniel in the best of health. After your first visit with your veterinarian, your dog will be placed on a regular, yearly vaccination schedule.

If your dog exhibits any of the following behaviors, you should definitely contact your veterinarian as soon as possible: Diarrhea, increased urination or vomiting for more than 12 hours; constipation or difficulty urinating; excessive discharge from nose, ears, and eyes; constant scratching; sneezing and coughing; loss of balance, fainting, shivering or limping; significant weight loss or increase; loss or increase of appetite for more than a day; drinking lots of water ; and sleeping too much or lack of normal energy.

Proper grooming is part of basic health care for your Springer. This is where you may have one of your first opportunities to discover anything unusual. In

Many veterinary offices are equipped with machines necessary to perform tests and get results the very same day you bring in your English Springer Spaniel.

addition, the attention you give your dog with proper and regular grooming shows your dog that you care for him. The importance of expressing your love for your dog is underrated, especially as it relates to your Springer's health.

Also often overlooked as important to your dog's basic health are a proper diet and regular exercise. In this respect, your Springer isn't so different from you!

A large percentage of dogs these days are overweight. This will inevitably reduce your dog's life span and increase the chances for your Springer to develop diseases related to being overweight. A proper diet and regular exercise should be enough to prevent this from happening. One way to

The veterinarian will check the inside of your Springer's mouth, and will also look for good strong teeth with no evidence of tartar build-up.

check if your dog is overweight is to stand directly over him, with your dog between your legs. Lean over and with both hands on him, move from front to back over his ribs. If you can feel his ribs without difficulty, he is probably fine. If you cannot feel his ribs without a little digging, he may need to lose some weight. Ask your veterinarian. If you cannot perform this check for your dog, perhaps you are overweight too!

English Springer Spaniels are generally very healthy dogs and are no more prone to certain diseases than other breeds. Nevertheless, there are some rare congenital diseases (diseases your dog is born with) that your

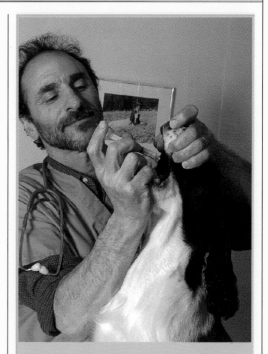

Some medications your English Springer Spaniel will receive will be oral. If this is a one-time treatment, your veterinarian may administer it, then you will not have to struggle with your pet.

Interdigital cysts and burrs are commonly found in between the toes of your English Springer Spaniel. You can check for these yourself with regular examinations at home.

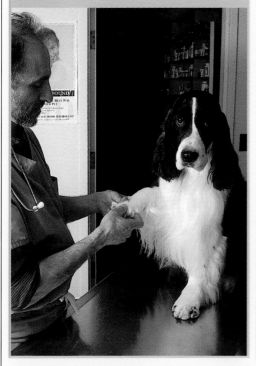

veterinarian may need to check for especially in Springers. They include: Factor XI deficiency (a problem with blood clotting); Ehlers-Danlos syndrome (very fragile skin that could result in serious lacerations with minimal damage); progressive retinal atrophy or PRA (causing loss of central vision); and unilateral or bilateral cryptorchidism (where one or both testicles do not descend from the abdomen). It is important to remember that even though these congenital disorders are serious, they are not very common in the breed.

There are other diseases that all dogs should be vaccinated against. These diseases are contagious (among dogs) as well

Next to you, your veterinarian will become your English Springer Spaniel's best friend.

Leptospirosis affects your dog's kidneys. It is caused by a kind of bacteria. Symptoms for both include fever and vomiting. A serious case of either disease can cause death. Again, vaccination is a very effective method of protection for your dog.

Parainfluenza ("kennel cough") affects your dog's windpipe and voicebox. It is caused by an airborne virus. Fortunately, the main symptom is coughing. However, it should still be treated as a serious problem and vaccinated against.

In United States and elsewhere, rabies is a well-known virus, to humans and dogs alike. It mostly affects the brain, causing severe damage in the process. The rabies virus is spread by infected saliva from an animal or person through

as preventable. Your English Springer Spaniel puppy will undergo a series of vaccinations for distemper, hepatitis, leptospirosis, parainfluenza, rabies and parvovirus. Your veterinarian will give you the most up-to-date information about the proper vaccination schedule for each.

Distemper can cause severe damage to your dog's nervous system, causing convulsions and paralysis. However, symptoms are varied. An airborne virus causes distemper, for which there is no known cure to date. Vaccination effectively protects your dog from this killer disease.

Hepatitis affects your dog's liver. It is caused by a virus that is spread by contact only.

Although the breeder you obtain your puppy from will guarantee his health, it is best to bring your new puppy to the veterinarian within 48 hours of bringing him home.

Your English Springer Spaniel puppy is dependent on you, his owner, to provide him with love and good care to keep him healthy. Any deviation from your puppy's normal actions should be cause for concern.

Early socialization begins with your English Springer Spaniel pup and his littermates. To continue socializing your puppy, you can enroll your pup in an obedience class.

Learn to take your dog's temperature. This is the first thing you should do if you think your English Springer Spaniel is feeling out of sorts.

It is easy for English Springer Spaniels to develop ear infections. Always check your dog's ears, and if there is a foul smell, contact your veterinarian immediately.

a bite wound. In dogs, symptoms may appear up to five days after a bite wound. Symptoms include a loosely hanging jaw and tongue, sometimes with a foaming mouth of saliva. There is currently no treatment for dogs with rabies, so vaccination is crucial.

Parvovirus affects the digestive system. It is caused by an intestinal virus and is spread through contaminated feces. Direct contact is not necessary for transmission of the virus. Symptoms include fever, vomiting, dehydration, and diarrhea, which may often contain blood. Death may occur, although there is currently no accurate measure of

Check your English Springer Spaniel's coat carefully during a bath for any external parasites like fleas or ticks.

detailed information about the most effective sprays, shampoos and other products available to kill these external parasites.

Fleas are very small and usually leave little dark spots behind on your dog's skin. Lice are also very small. Both are easy to detect with careful examination, especially if your dog is scratching more than usual. This includes mites as well, which are even smaller than fleas and lice! There are many kinds of mites that affect different parts of your dog's body, from the ears to the skin.

If you do find fleas on your dog, make sure to inspect his sleeping area, and other parts of the house your dog frequents. As with lice, fleas usually are not just contained to your dog. Then

the mortality rate. Vaccination is a must.

Another major area of concern regarding your English Springer Spaniel's health are parasites, both external and internal. External parasites include fleas, ticks, lice and mites. Internal parasites include roundworms, hookworms, whipworms, tapeworms and heartworms. Currently, there are no long-lasting treatments to keep parasites away, such as a vaccine. However, there are many effective treatments for all of them.

All external parasites are blood-suckers. They can spread many diseases, including some internal parasites, in addition to causing severe skin irritation and allergic reactions themselves. Your veterinarian can give you more

Keep your English Springer Spaniel's nails trimmed to the proper length so that his movement is not hindered in any way.

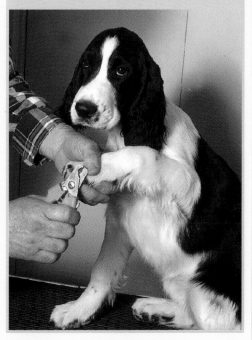

CAT FLEA - FEEDING

The cat flea is the most common flea of both dogs and cats. These are easily pick up from the outdoors, but not so easy to eradicate.

and can reach sizes over a foot long! They are spread by female mosquitoes that bite a contaminated dog and transmit it to the next unlucky dog they bite.

Heartworms are a very serious problem. Heart failure, in addition to complications to your dog's lungs and kidneys, are all

there's the giant mites, also known as ticks. Unlike fleas and lice, ticks are usually not as widespread a problem, though hunting dogs are more prone to these because of their exposure to wooded areas (where ticks live).

Unfortunately, all these internal parasites are fairly common as well as difficult to get rid of. Repeated treatments are usually necessary before any hope of full recovery. Most look like small pieces of rice or spaghetti when found in your dog's feces. Many cause loss of blood, threatening your dog's general health. Contact your veterinarian immediately if you suspect your dog is contaminated.

The only internal parasite that does not live in your dog's digestive system is the heartworm. As its name implies, it lives in your dog's heart once it reaches maturity. Heartworms can survive in your dog's heart sometimes for up to five years,

If you discover your English Springer Spaniel has fleas, everything must be treated within his living space. This includes your furniture, carpeting, all bedding, etc.

possible dangers of advanced heartworm infestation. There are preventive medications available, as well as medications that effectively get rid of heartworms. Ask your veterinarian about blood tests to detect heartworms and about medications available to prevent heartworms, which can be administered daily or monthly.

If your English Springer Spaniel does require medicine, either in liquid or pill form, administering the medicine should be easy. Probably the best method is to mix or hide it with his food or a treat. However, some dogs may detect it and refuse to eat it. In this case, you should just administer the medicine directly into your dog's mouth.

Talk to your dog calmly, put your hand over his muzzle, and then lift the sides of his mouth open. Place the pill in the back of

After every time your English Springer is to come in from the outdoors, it is advisable to give his coat a quick once-over to check for fleas and ticks.

his mouth. Close his mouth and hold his muzzle upwards, stroking his throat until he swallows. With liquid, place the dropper into the

While your English Springer Spaniel will love spending time in the great outdoors, there are many potential hazards that responsible owners must safeguard against.

Get your new English Springer puppy set on a health schedule with your veterinarian as soon as possible. Your puppy's good health and longevity is directly related to the amount of time and good care you give to him.

corner of his mouth between his back teeth and administer the medicine. Keep your dog's mouth shut until he swallows.

Another important area of health care that doesn't get as much attention as it should is the subject of spaying and neutering. Spaying and neutering are surgical procedures that permanently alter your dog so he or she can not reproduce. Spaying your female dog involves removal of her ovaries and uterus. Neutering your male dog involves removal of his testicles.

Spaying and neutering do not make your dog fat or lazy. Your dog's behavior will not change for the worse. Spaying and neutering are permanent methods of birth control and have some very positive side effects. Uterine

Spaying/neutering is often the best option for your family pet. The health benefits are numerous and it will minimize the risk of certain diseases.

infection and mammary cancer are two diseases your female dog will not be susceptible to after being spayed. Prostate cancer is one of the diseases your male dog will be less susceptible to after being neutered.

If you are not going to breed your English Springer Spaniel puppy or dog, please get her spayed or him neutered! It will benefit your dog and will most certainly prevent an increase in the population of unwanted puppies and dogs that fill shelters and humane societies everywhere.

Breeding is best left to those who are experienced and truly interested in improving the breed. Rarely does a breeder ever make money in the process. Most will tell you that when all is said and done, they have usually lost money. In addition, there is also the large amount of time you will spend taking care of a litter of newborn puppies to consider. That responsibility should not end when the puppies leave you after two months. Responsible breeders do what they do for the love of the breed and are always available to all their adoptive families for advice. If you still believe that you would like to find out more about breeding your Springer, do your research. Talk to breeders, and read as much as you can before making your final decision.

Making sure your English Springer Spaniel has the proper health care is an important part of being a responsible owner. It involves a partnership with your veterinarian. More importantly, it involves a commitment from you to be your dog's best friend. That's only fair, isn't it? After all, your Springer is your best friend for as long he lives!

Breeding should only be attempted by someone who is conscientious, knowledgeable and willing to take responsibility for the dogs involved and the new puppies.

SUGGESTED READING

THE MOST COMPLETE DOG BOOK EVER WRITTEN
(a Canine Lexicon)
by Andrew DePrisco and James B. Johnson
TS-175
896 pages, over 1300 full color photographs.

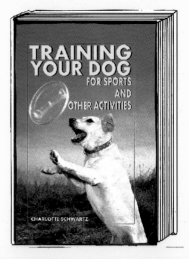

TRAINING YOUR DOG FOR SPORTS AND OTHER ACTIVITIES
by Charlotte Schwartz
TS-258
160 pages, over 200 full color photographs.

A NEW OWNER'S GUIDE TO ENGLISH SPRINGER SPANIELS
by Art Perle
JG-114
160 pages, over 125 full color photographs.

OWNER'S GUIDE TO DOG HEALTH
by Lowell Ackerman, DVM
TS-214
432 pages, over 300 color photographs.